DISCOVERING THE UNITED STATES

Montana

BY HEATHER BODE

Kids Core

An Imprint of Abdo Publishing
abdobooks.com

abdobooks.com

Published by Abdo Publishing, a division of ABDO, PO Box 398166, Minneapolis, Minnesota 55439. Copyright © 2025 by Abdo Consulting Group, Inc. International copyrights reserved in all countries. No part of this book may be reproduced in any form without written permission from the publisher. Kids Core™ is a trademark and logo of Abdo Publishing.

Printed in the United States of America, North Mankato, Minnesota.
052024
092024

THIS BOOK CONTAINS RECYCLED MATERIALS

Cover Photo: Katie Berdan Wolden/iStockphoto
Interior Photos: Bettmann/Getty Images, 4–5; Brian Lasenby/Shutterstock Images, 7 (top left); Dominic Gentilcore PhD/Shutterstock Images, 7 (top right); iStockphoto, 7 (bottom left), 8; Shutterstock Images, 7 (bottom right), 12; Heeb Christian/Prisma by Dukas Presseagentur GmbH/Alamy, 10–11; Heidi Besen/Shutterstock Images, 15; John Lambing/Alamy, 16; Mihai Andritoiu/Alamy, 18–19; Ignacio Palacios/Stone/Getty Images, 21; Jordan Siemens/Stone/Getty Images, 22; George Ostertag/Alamy, 24; Chuck Haney/Danita Delimont/Alamy, 25; Zack Frank/Shutterstock Images, 26; Hugh K. Telleria/Shutterstock Images, 28 (top left); Snehit Photo/Shutterstock Images, 28 (top right); Matt Champlin/The Image Bank Unreleased/Getty Images, 28 (bottom); Red Line Editorial, 29 (top), 29 (bottom)

Editor: Christa Kelly
Series Design: Katharine Hale

Library of Congress Control Number: 2023949352

Publisher's Cataloging-in-Publication Data

Names: Bode, Heather, author.
Title: Montana / by Heather Bode
Description: Minneapolis, Minnesota: Abdo Publishing, 2025 | Series: Discovering the United States | Includes online resources and index.
Identifiers: ISBN 9781098293963 (lib. bdg.) | ISBN 9798384913238 (ebook)
Subjects: LCSH: U.S. states--Juvenile literature. | Montana--History--Juvenile literature. | Western States (U.S.)--Juvenile literature. | Physical geography--United States--Juvenile literature.
Classification: DDC 973--dc23

All population data taken from:
"Estimates of Population by Sex, Race, and Hispanic Origin: April 1, 2020 to July 1, 2022." *US Census Bureau, Population Division,* June 2023, census.gov.

CONTENTS

Barnum Brown was digging in an area known as the Hell Creek Formation, a place known for its many fossils.

CHAPTER 1

Tyrannosaurus Rex

In 1902, Barnum Brown was looking for **fossils** in northern Montana. One day, he found something special. It was the remains of a huge dinosaur with sharp teeth! Brown had never seen anything like it. He kept digging.

It took three years of dusting bones and blasting rocks to free the fossil. When he finished, Brown knew he had discovered a new dinosaur. He had found the first remains of a *Tyrannosaurus rex* (*T. rex*).

Montana's Land

Montana is the fourth largest US state by area. It is in the US region called the West. Canada borders Montana to the north. Idaho borders

Triple Divide Peak

Montana is home to a mountain called Triple Divide Peak. The peak's rain and snow drain into the Pacific, Atlantic, and Arctic Oceans. It is the only mountain in the United States that drains into three different oceans.

Montana Facts

Western meadowlark

Ponderosa pine

STATE FLOWER

STATE MAMMAL

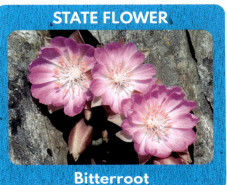

Bitterroot

Grizzly bear

DATE OF STATEHOOD
November 8, 1889

CAPITAL
Helena

POPULATION
1,139,507

AREA
147,040 square miles
(380,8302 sq km)

Each US state has a different population, size, and capital city. States also have state symbols.

the state to the west. Wyoming lies to the south. To the east are North Dakota and South Dakota.

Western Montana is covered in mountains. The Rocky Mountains are among the most famous. They cover two-fifths of Montana.

Montana has more than 100 mountain ranges.

The mountains are snow-capped most of the year. Flat grasslands cover central Montana. Eastern Montana is home to the Badlands. This is a region with colorful rock formations. Very little grows in the Badlands.

Montana's Climate

Montana has long, cold winters. The mountains get a lot of snow. In higher **elevations**, snow can fall any month of the year. In the spring,

Montana gets a lot of rain. Summers in Montana are hot, but there is little moisture in the air. This makes the temperature feel pleasant. Leaves change color in the fall.

Many plants and animals thrive in Montana. Ponderosa pine trees grow across the state. Small, pink flowers called bitterroots grow in rocky soil at high elevations. Grizzly bears feast on huckleberries.

Explore Online

Visit the website below. Does it give any new information about Montana that was not mentioned in Chapter 1?

Montana

abdocorelibrary.com/discovering -montana

Every year, members of the Crow Nation host a powwow to celebrate their heritage.

CHAPTER 2

The People of Montana

American Indians were the first people to live in Montana. The land is home to many nations, including the Blackfeet, Kootenai, and Crow. Each nation has its own culture and traditions. Many people from these nations still live in Montana today.

Montana's state flag includes the words *Oro y Plata*. This means "Gold and Silver."

In 1858, three **prospectors** found gold in western Montana. Miners also found silver and copper. Some found gems such as sapphires and garnets. Montana became known as the Treasure State.

Over the next few decades, more than 10,000 people traveled to Montana to look for treasure. They forced American Indian nations to give up their land. The US government made some American Indians live on small sections of land called reservations. Other American Indians were forced to leave the state.

Montana Today

Today, 6.5 percent of people in Montana are American Indian. Almost 89 percent are white.

Ghost Towns

Montana has many ghost towns. These are abandoned towns. When gold or other resources ran out, people had to move somewhere else. The buildings remain standing. Ghost towns help modern visitors learn about the past.

About 4.5 percent are Hispanic or Latino. A little more than 1 percent are Asian. Less than 1 percent are Black.

Many people in Montana enjoy spending time outside. In warm weather, they hike and mountain bike. They go camping and boating. They ski and snowmobile in winter.

Fishing is another popular activity in Montana. Trout is a popular fish to catch. The fish can be baked, grilled, or fried.

Working in Montana

Many people in Montana work in the energy **industry**. They provide the country with coal, crude oil, and natural gas. These natural resources are used as fuel. Montana also

Montana is home to more than a dozen ski resorts.

produces renewable energy. The state has several sites that make **hydroelectric power**.

Some people in Montana work as farmers. Many raise cows for their meat. Others raise bison. Bison meat is less fatty than cow meat.

Bison are the largest land mammals in North America.

The meat can be turned into bison burgers. Farmers also grow crops such as wheat.

Mining is another important industry in Montana. People mine for precious metals and gems. Others work in the tourism industry. Many people visit Montana to see its beautiful mountains and rock formations.

Before Montana became a state, the government sent people to examine the land. Newspapers printed part of the report in 1867:

> Veins of gold, silver, copper, lead, and iron are found in great numbers in nearly all the mountainous portions of the Territory. . . . Her mines . . . will prove as rich and yield as large profits as the most productive in this or any other country.

Source: "Surveyor General's Report." *The Richmond Palladium*, 5 Dec. 1867, *Library of Congress*, loc.gov. Accessed 4 Sept. 2023.

What's the Big Idea?

Read this quote. What's the main idea? Explain how the main idea is supported by details.

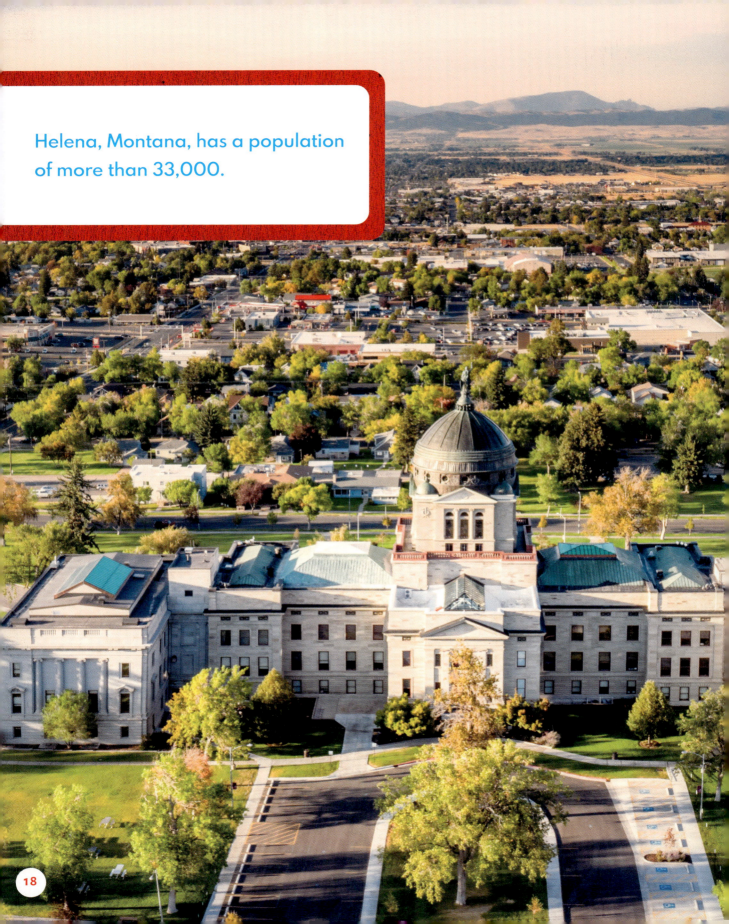

Helena, Montana, has a population of more than 33,000.

CHAPTER 3

Places in Montana

Helena is the capital of Montana. The city used to be a gold mining town. Visitors can learn about the capital's history at the Montana Historical Society.

Billings is the most **populated** city in Montana. It is an important place for the state's businesses.

The city has several sites that turn oil into products such as gas. Farmers also sell their livestock in Billings.

Bozeman is another popular city. The city is home to the Museum of the Rockies. This museum has many dinosaur fossils. Visitors can watch workers brush and chip away at newly found fossils.

Parks

Montana shares Yellowstone National Park with Idaho and Wyoming. Yellowstone has hot springs, **geysers**, and boiling mud pots. The park is also rich in wildlife. Visitors can see herds of bison and elk. They may also spot wolves and moose.

Bacteria makes Yellowstone's hot springs multicolored.

About 3 million tourists visit Glacier National Park each year.

Glacier National Park is in northwestern Montana. The park is famous for its glaciers. Glaciers are slow-moving slabs of ice. The park is also well-known for its natural beauty. It has many waterfalls, lakes, and mountain peaks. Bighorn sheep, mountain goats, and grizzly bears roam the land.

Montana also has 55 state parks. The biggest is Makoshika State Park in eastern Montana.

The Continental Divide

The Continental Divide runs through Glacier National Park. The divide stretches from Alaska to Mexico. Rivers to the west of the divide empty into the Pacific Ocean. Rivers to the east flow to the Atlantic Ocean.

Makoshika's visitor center was created to display the park's *Triceratops horridus* skull.

The park's visitor center has a *T. rex* and a *Triceratops horridus* fossil on display. Both fossils were found in the park.

Pictograph Cave State Park is located in southern Montana. Thousands of years ago,

The pictographs in Pictograph Cave State Park depict animals, warriors, and weapons.

ancient humans lived in the park's caves. They left thousands of ancient tools and weapons. They also left **pictographs** on the cave walls. More recent pictographs were added by American Indians in the last few centuries. Many of the pictographs are still visible today.

William Clark and his guide Sacagawea visited Pompeys Pillar in 1806.

Landmarks

Pompeys Pillar is an important landmark in southern Montana. It is a 120-foot (37-m) tall rock formation. The pillar is covered in thousands of American Indian pictographs. It was also signed by Captain William Clark, an American who explored the western United States.

The Little Bighorn Battlefield is another important landmark. In 1876, several American

Indian nations fought the US Army. They refused to leave their land. After a deadly battle, the American Indians won. The Little Bighorn Battlefield National Monument marks the place of the battle.

Treasure can be many things. Some people say it is gold and gems. Others say treasure is clean water and scenic mountains. Whatever treasure means to someone, it can be found in Montana.

Further Evidence

Look at the website below. Does it give any new evidence to support Chapter Three?

Montana

abdocorelibrary.com/discovering -montana

State Map

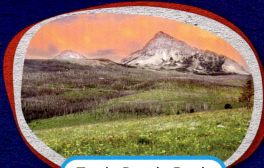

Triple Divide Peak

Museum of the Rockies

Little Bighorn Battlefield

Montana: The Treasure State

CANADA

Glacier National Park

Triple Divide Peak

Flathead Lake

ROCKY MOUNTAINS

Missouri River

Fort Peck Lake

HELL CREEK FORMATION

Makoshika State Park

North Dakota

Missoula

Great Falls

Helena

Billings

Pompeys Pillar

Little Bighorn Battlefield

Butte

Bozeman

Yellowstone River

Pictograph Cave State Park

South Dakota

N W E S

Yellowstone National Park

Idaho

Wyoming

KEY

⭐ Capital   🪧 Park

🔵 City or town   📌 Point of interest

Glossary

elevations
heights above sea level

fossil
the very old, preserved remains of an animal or plant

geysers
hot springs that occasionally shoot water into the air

hydroelectric power
electricity made using moving water

industry
a group of businesses that serve similar purposes

pictographs
ancient drawings, often found on rock walls

populated
settled or lived in

prospectors
people who prospect, or search, for precious minerals and metals in new areas

Online Resources

To learn more about Montana, visit our free resource websites below.

Visit **abdocorelibrary.com** or scan this QR code for free Common Core resources for teachers and students, including vetted activities, multimedia, and booklinks, for deeper subject comprehension.

Visit **abdobooklinks.com** or scan this QR code for free additional online weblinks for further learning. These links are routinely monitored and updated to provide the most current information available.

Learn More

Hall, Ashley. *Fossils for Kids*. Rockridge, 2020.

Lehmann, Steph. *Montana History for Kids in 50 Objects*. Farcountry, 2021.

Payne, Stefanie. *The National Parks*. DK, 2020.

Index

About the Author

Heather L. Bode is an elementary educator who has taught in South Dakota, Montana, and Minnesota. She has family roots in Billings, Butte, and Helena, Montana. She loves to travel and camp with her family. She currently lives in Minneapolis, Minnesota.